A-Minute-A-Day High Frequency Words

2019 US Edition

40 Photocopiable One Minute Challenges
to Improve Reading Skills.

A Teacher Timesaver by Sheila Crompton

dp

DEBRICH PUBLISHING

2019
PUBLISHED BY
DEBRICH PUBLISHING,
LOCHSIDE FARM, SANQUHAR, DUMFRIESSHIRE.
DG4 6EW.

2nd Edition © DEBRICH PUBLISHING 2019

The purchase of this book entitles the purchaser to reproduce photo-copies or stencil duplicates of the black-line masters for immediate teaching purposes within their own establishment.

Copying, storing or transmitting this publication in whole or part for any other purpose is strictly prohibited without the prior written permission of the publisher.

A catalogue record of this book has been lodged and is available from the British Library.

ISBN 978-1-9160466-0-3

WHAT IS A MINUTE A DAY?

A-MINUTE-A-DAY is a series of 3 books, which aim to improve basic reading and mental maths skills, in a challenging yet fun way.

Each book contains a number of photocopiable games, each focusing upon specific groups of letters, words or numbers.

The aim of each game is for the student to give as many correct verbal answers as possible within 1 minute. **No writing skills are required.**

Each page or worksheet can be used repeatedly by the student for practice both in school and at home, and progress assessed by the teacher in just A-MINUTE-A-DAY.

WHY A-MINUTE-A-DAY?

A-MINUTE-A-DAY has at its roots, a method known as **precision teaching,** which since its inception in 1964, has been adopted by an ever increasing number of teachers, and its proven success in both mainstream and special needs education is indisputable.

The value of precision teaching lies in identifying a specific area of need for a particular child, followed by a daily period of teaching, testing and evaluating progress.

Normally, this process can take around 10-15 minutes of completely undivided attention for a particular child. Whilst this can be considered a short enough period to offer any child, for a teacher without ancillary support and with multiple children requiring similar help, it can often be impossible to achieve.

A-MINUTE-A-DAY offers a new methodology, which enables teachers to offer their students tailored systematic practice and monitoring of progress on a daily basis, whilst drastically reducing the amount of teacher involvement.

A-MINUTE-A-DAY HIGH FREQUENCY WORDS

In order for children to become fluent readers, it is essential that they are able to read words both in and out of context. It may be possible for them to decipher unfamiliar words using phonic skills but phonically irregular words may disrupt the flow of the reader and thus hinder fluency.

* Research has shown that the 25 most common words make up about one third of all printed material and in addition, there is a group of around 100 words which comprise approximately 50% of all the words likely to be encountered.

These are known as *high frequency words.* Mastery will provide a firm foundation upon which reading competence may be achieved. In addition to the first 100 high frequency words, for a child to be a fluent reader, it is recommended that mastery of a further 120 words be included .

A-MINUTE-A-DAY HIGH FREQUENCY WORDS supports this approach to reading and

in addition to focusing upon the first 220 essential words, further widens the pupil's sight vocabulary by including groups of words based around specific themes.

•Source: The Reading Teacher's Book of Lists, Fourth Edition, © 2000 by Prentice Hall Authors: Fry,
•Kress & Fountoukidis.

KEY FEATURES OF A-MINUTE-A-DAY

ENCOURAGES PARENTAL INVOLVEMENT

So many teachers battle stoically on, alone, and yet there is a vast and frequently untapped source of support in the form of parents and family who are invariably eager and capable of participating in their child's education.

FUN - YET CHALLENGING. EVERY CHILD CAN ENJOY SUCCESS.

Parents want their children to learn, so let us show them how they can help, but LET IT BE FUN, not with tedious lists, but with games. Above all, let us ensure that homework at Primary level is a shared experience for parent and child.

SAVES HOURS OF HOMEWORK PREPARATION AND MARKING

Often, there is insufficient time to set homework on a regular basis for primary children, and still less time to check it. If therefore, there is some way in which teachers could direct parents to an area of need for their child, which they would practise for no more than 10 minutes a night, all that is required of the teacher, is A-MINUTE-A-DAY to monitor the child's progress.

IMPROVEMENT IS MEASURABLE AND EASILY UNDERSTOOD BY THE CHILD

Children love competition - provided that the pressure is not too great. Let them compete against themselves. If they can answer six questions one night, make sure they can answer eight the next, and so on. It does not matter where you begin, it's how much you improve that counts.
Often the slowest children are able to enjoy the most success, because they have the room for the greatest improvement.

SPEED + ACCURACY = FLUENCY

Each game requires the child to give 30 correct *verbal responses* within 1 minute. This gives adequate opportunity for accurate responses. There is little value in encouraging speed at the expense of accuracy. As the child becomes more skilful, and the first goal is achieved, the time limit may be reduced. For most of the games, a time limit of thirty seconds should not be beyond the ability of the average child.

BLANK GAMES TO SUPPORT FURTHER VOCABULARY WORK.

Included at the end of the book are five content- free games, which may be used by the teacher to offer additional words to suit an individual child, or to offer a game with high repetition for children who learn at a slower pace..

Sheila Crompton 2019

CONTENTS

RECEPTION

1. EGGS	2. BUBBLES	3. SHELLS	4. LITTLE DOG	5. RAINDROPS
I	are	big	it	he
go	the	she	at	am
come	of	and	play	all
went	we	they	no	is
up	this	my	yes	cat
you	dog	see	for	get
day	me	on	a	said
was	like	away	dad	to
look	going	mum	can	in

YRS 1-2

6. SAVE	7. BALLOON RACE	8. DUCK RACE	9. LUCKY DIP	10. JAM TARTS
about	may	with	home	too
can't	people	an	must	pocket
her	there	do	put	back
many	will	his	time	ball
over	again	much	your	door
then	did	pull	as	how
who	him	three	dig	new
after	more	would	house	saw
could	push	another	name	took
ere	these	don't	ran	rabbit

YRS 1-2

11. BUTTERFLY	12. HOT X BUNS	13. PUDDLES	14. GARDEN PATH	15 PARTY TIME
down	seen	bed	making	brother
if	two	girl	got	had
next	lived	last	boy	live [d]
school	because	now	little	once
tree	from	say[s]	old	way
carrot	just	been	off	but
be	not	very	so	half
first	should	good	want	love
jump	us	laugh	some	one
night	called	having	water	take

YEARS 4-5

16. EGG HUNT	17. STARLIGHT	18. SNOW STORM	19. ORANGES	20. BUILD A WALL
by	make	ask [ed]	goes	leaves [ing]
has	our	began	gone	show
made	their	being	heard	started
or	when	brought	I'm	stopped
that	came	change	jumped	think
what	help	coming	knew	thought
call [ed]	man	didn't	know	told
have	out	does	leave	tries
than	them	don't	might	turn [ed]
were	where	found	opened	used

CONTENTS [cont]

YEARS 4-5

21. AGILITY CLASS	22. FLASH CARDS	23. FEATHERS	24. LADYBIRD	25. BOOKS
watch	first	still	along	near
write	half	suddenly	also	other
woke[n]	morning	today	around	outside
almost	much	until	below	place
always	never	upon	between	right
any	number	while	both	round
before	often	year	different	such
better	only	young	follow [ing]	through
during	second	above	high	together
every	sometimes	across	inside	under

YEARS 4-5

26. KITES	27. SWALLOWS	28. BIKE RACE	29. SCRABBLE	30. DAYS
where	happy	earth	walk [ed] [ing]	Monday
without	head	eyes	paper	Tuesday
baby	heard	father	sister	Wednesday
balloon	something	friends	small	Thursday
birthday	sure	important	sound	Friday
brother	swimming	lady	white	Saturday
children	those	light	whole	Sunday
clothes	word	money	why	
garden	hear [ing]	mother	window	
great	work [ed] [ing]	world	own	

YEARS 4-5

31. MONTHS	32. NOS. 1-10	33. NOS. 11-20	34. COLORS	35. QUESTIONS
January	one	eleven	red	who
February	two	twelve	blue	where
March2/ May2	three	thirteen	yellow	when
April	four	fourteen	green	which
June2/July2	five	fifteen	purple	why
August	six	sixteen	orange	how
September	seven	seventeen	brown	what
October	eight	eighteen	black	
November	nine	nineteen	white	
December	ten	twenty	pink	

CONTENT FREE

36. HOME ADDRESS	37. SCHOOL	38. HOOFPRINTS	39. MOTOCROSS	40. TRAFFIC JAM

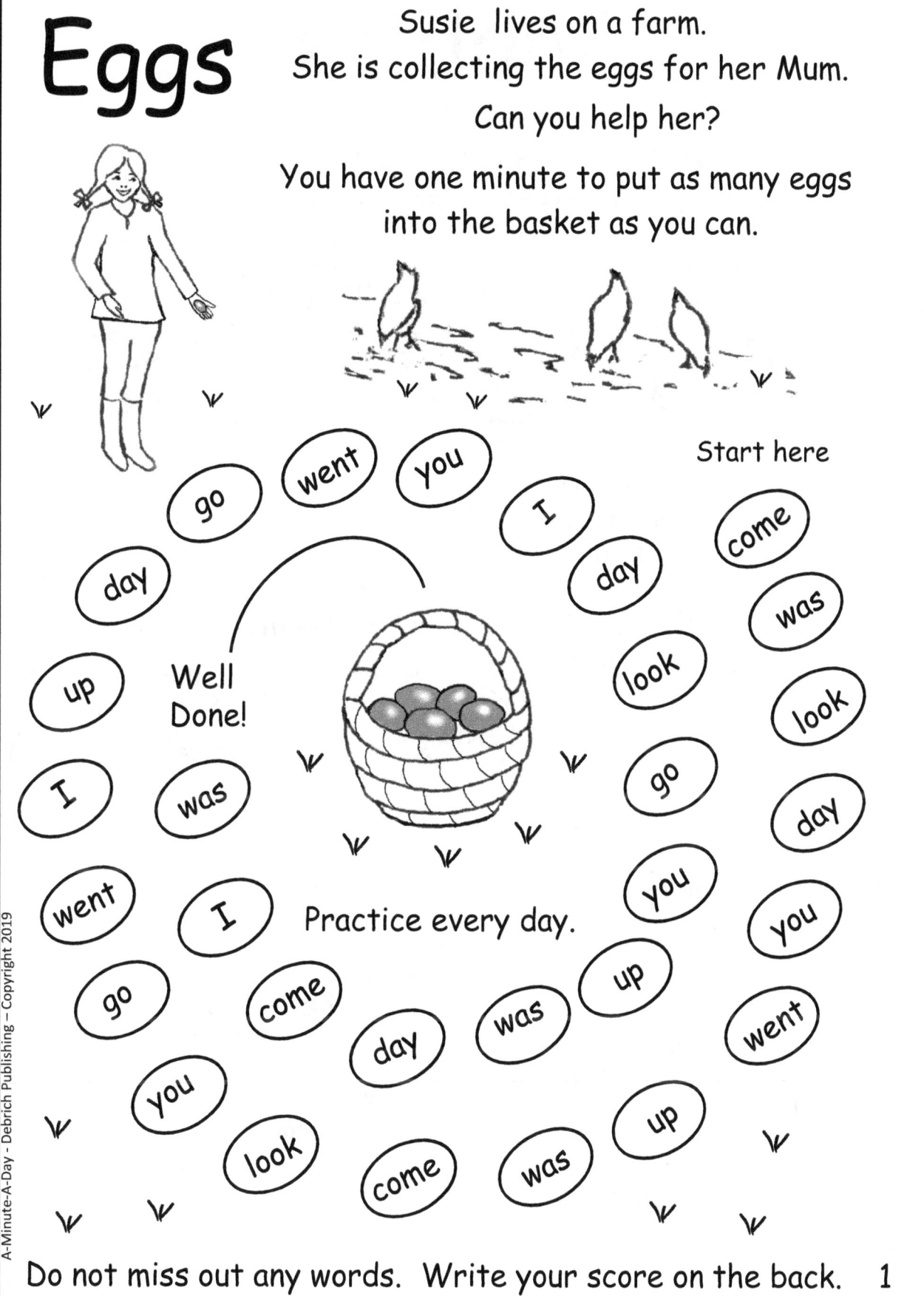

Bubbles

Sam likes to blow bubbles.
His dog Jack likes to jump up and pop the bubbles!
How many bubbles can you read before Jack pops them?

You have one minute to try.

Do not miss any words

Practice every day.

Write your score on the back

dog, are, this, going, me, like, of, are, going, me, dog, the, we, this, of, the, this, we, like, going, of, are, we, this, like, are, dog, going!, me

2

Shells

Ken and Jill are hunting for shells..
Can you help them?

You may pick up a shell if you can read the word.
Hurry – in just one minute, the tide will come in!

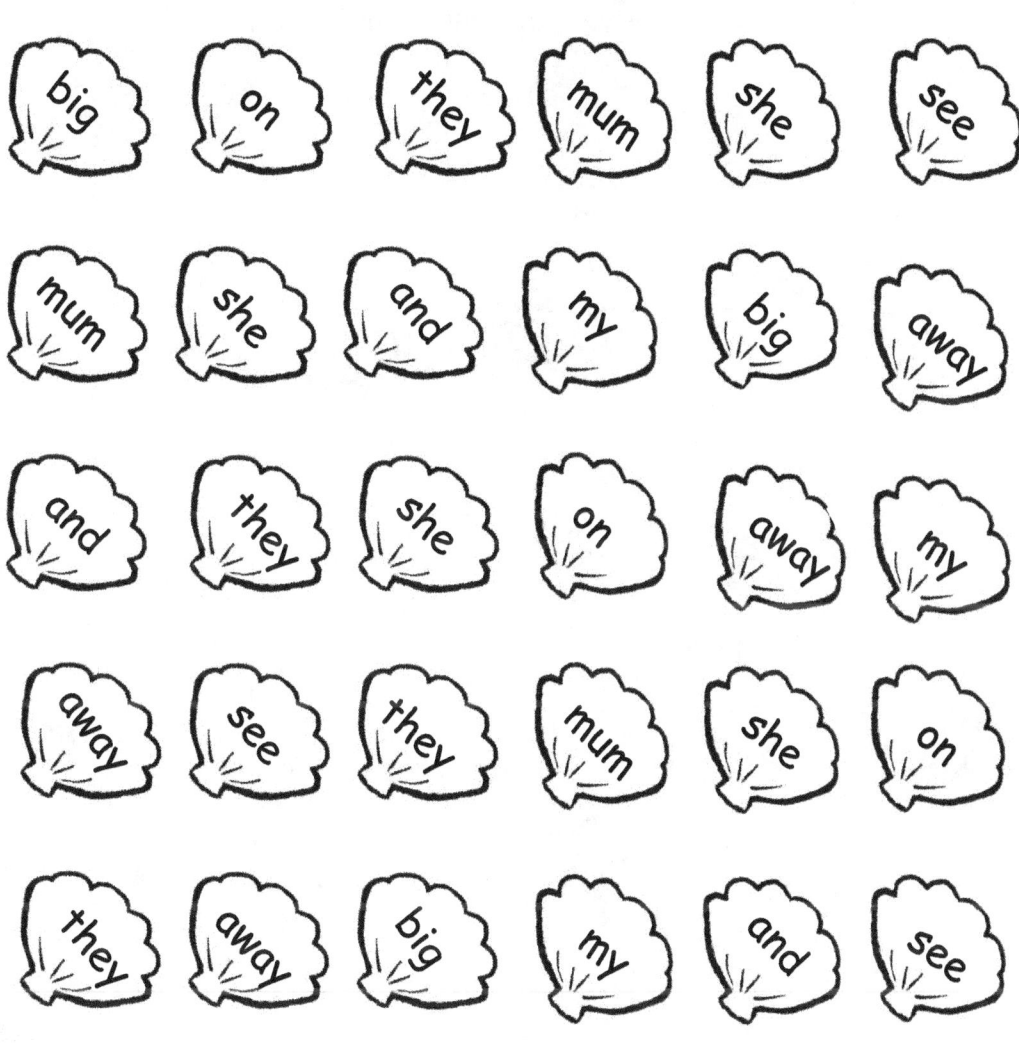

Practice every day.
Do not miss out any words.
Write your score on the back.

Little Dog

"Oh where, oh where has my little dog gone?
Oh where, oh where can he be?
With his ears so short and his tail so long,
Oh where, oh where is he?"

Can you follow the paw prints to find the dog?
You will need to hurry, in case he runs away again!
You have just one minute to try.

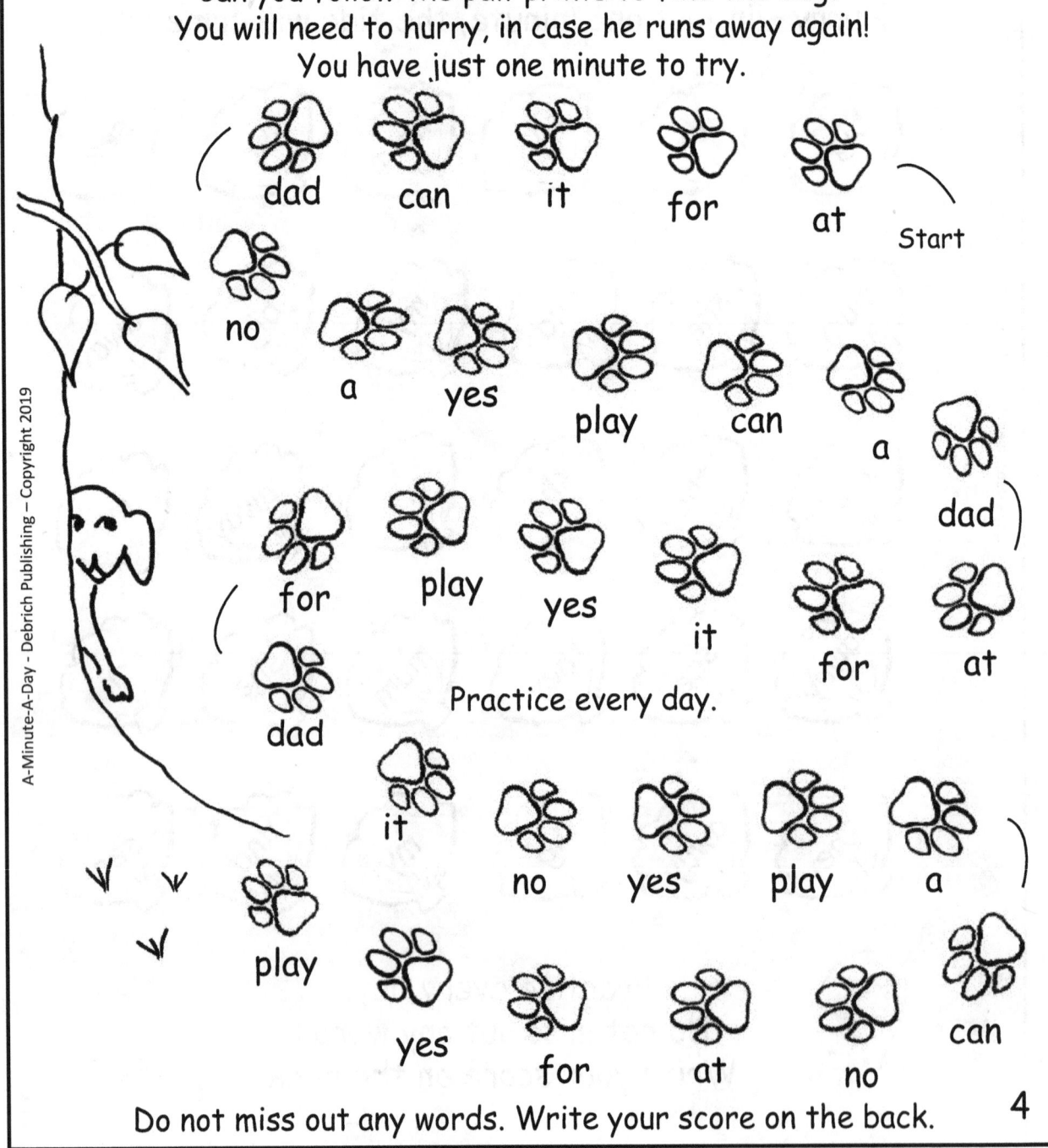

Practice every day.

Do not miss out any words. Write your score on the back.

Save!

Joe plays football for the school team.
He is a brilliant goalie!
You have just one minute
to see how many goals you can get past him.

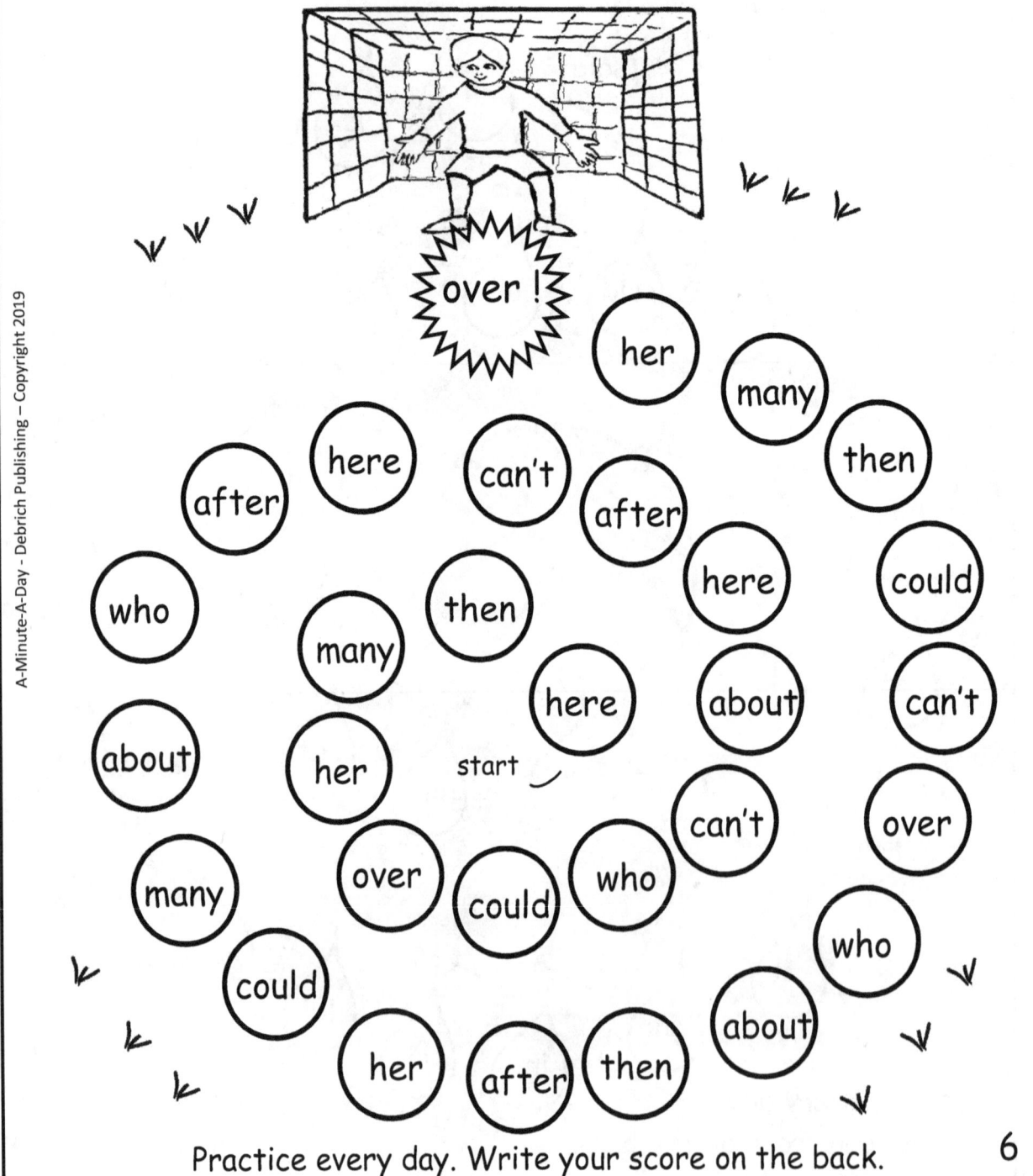

Practice every day. Write your score on the back.

Balloon Race

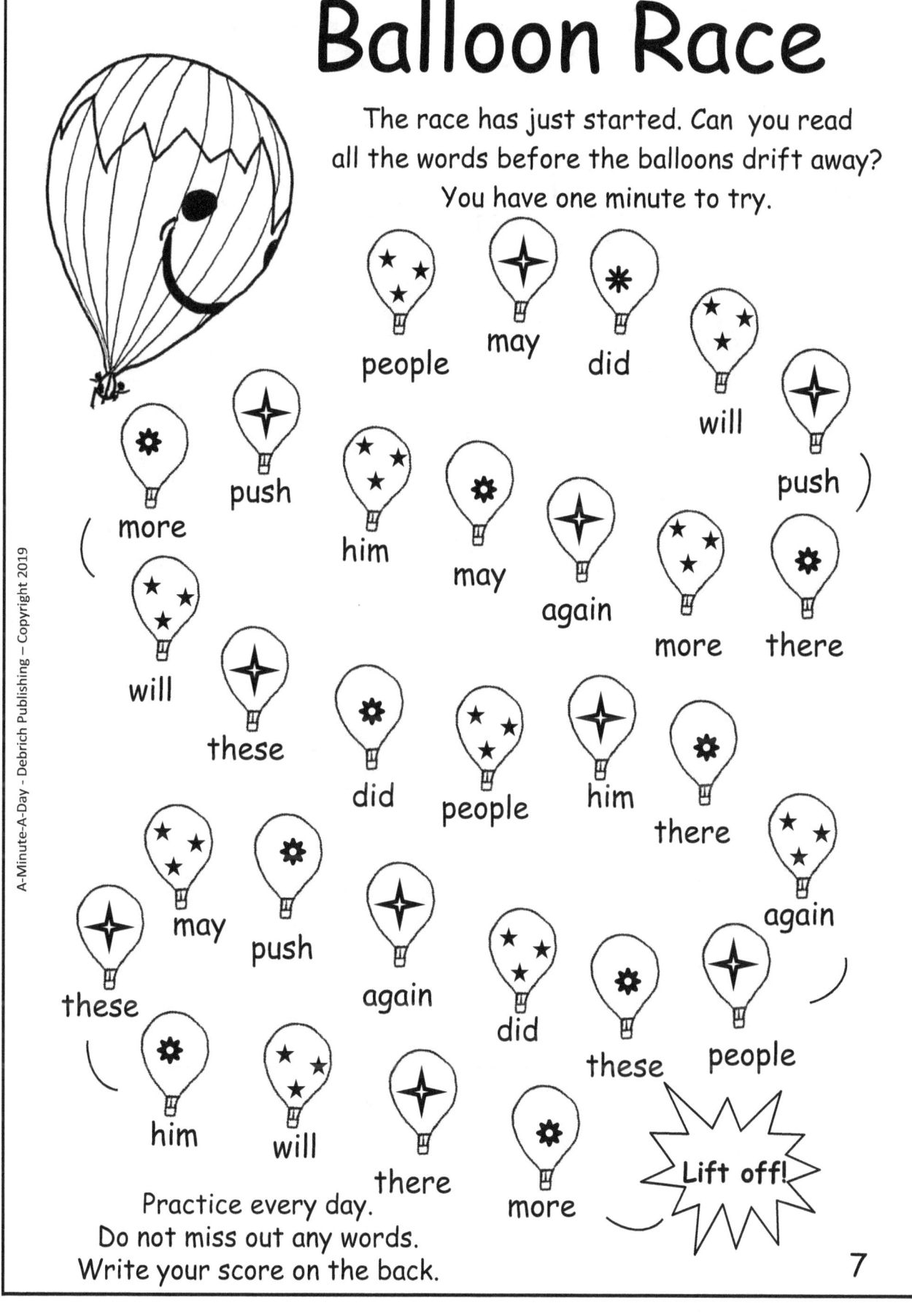

The race has just started. Can you read all the words before the balloons drift away? You have one minute to try.

people may did will push more push him may again more there will these did people him there may push again did these again people him will there more Lift off!

Practice every day.
Do not miss out any words.
Write your score on the back.

Lucky Dip

It is the school Summer Fair.
The children will win a prize
if they can read the name on the parcel.
Can you help them?

You have one minute to read them all.

house	must	home	put	time
your	as	name	house	dig
must	ran	time	home	put
name	your	dig	as	ran
dig	house	ran	must	name
as	home	put	your	time

Practice every day.
Do not miss out any words. Write your score on the back.

Jam Tarts

The Queen of Hearts
She made some tarts,
All on a summer's day.
The Knave of Hearts
He stole those tarts,
And took them clean away.

Can you chase the Knave and get the Queen's tarts back?
Hurry, he is a fast runner and will be gone in 1 minute!

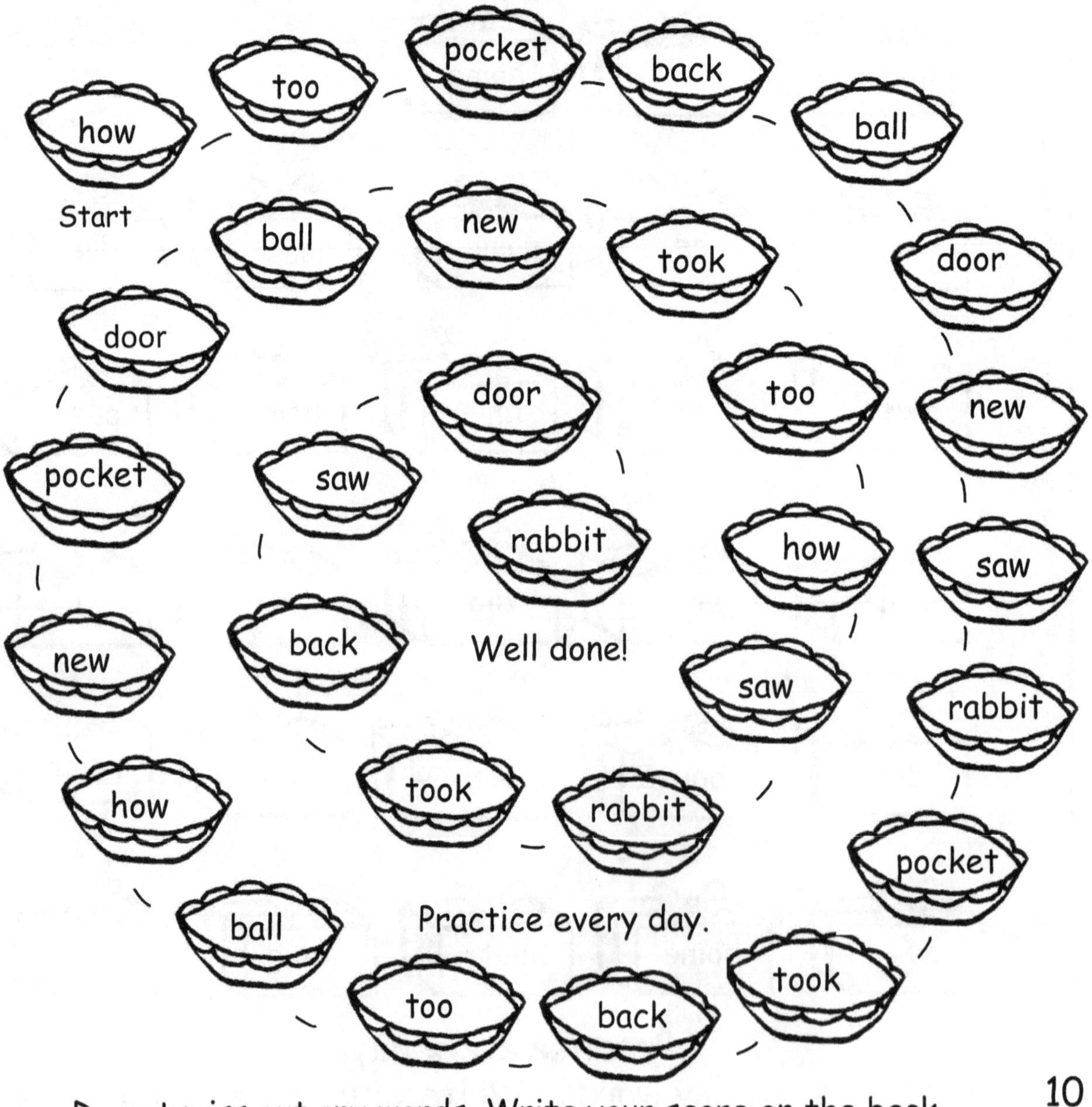

Start: how → too → pocket → back → ball → door → new → took → door → ball → door → saw → too → new → pocket → rabbit → how → saw → new → back → saw → rabbit → how → took → rabbit → pocket → ball → too → back → took — Well done!

Practice every day.

Do not miss out any words. Write your score on the back.

Butterfly

The butterfly is sipping nectar from each flower
but she may only visit a flower if she can read the word.
Can you help her?
You have one minute to read as many words as you can.

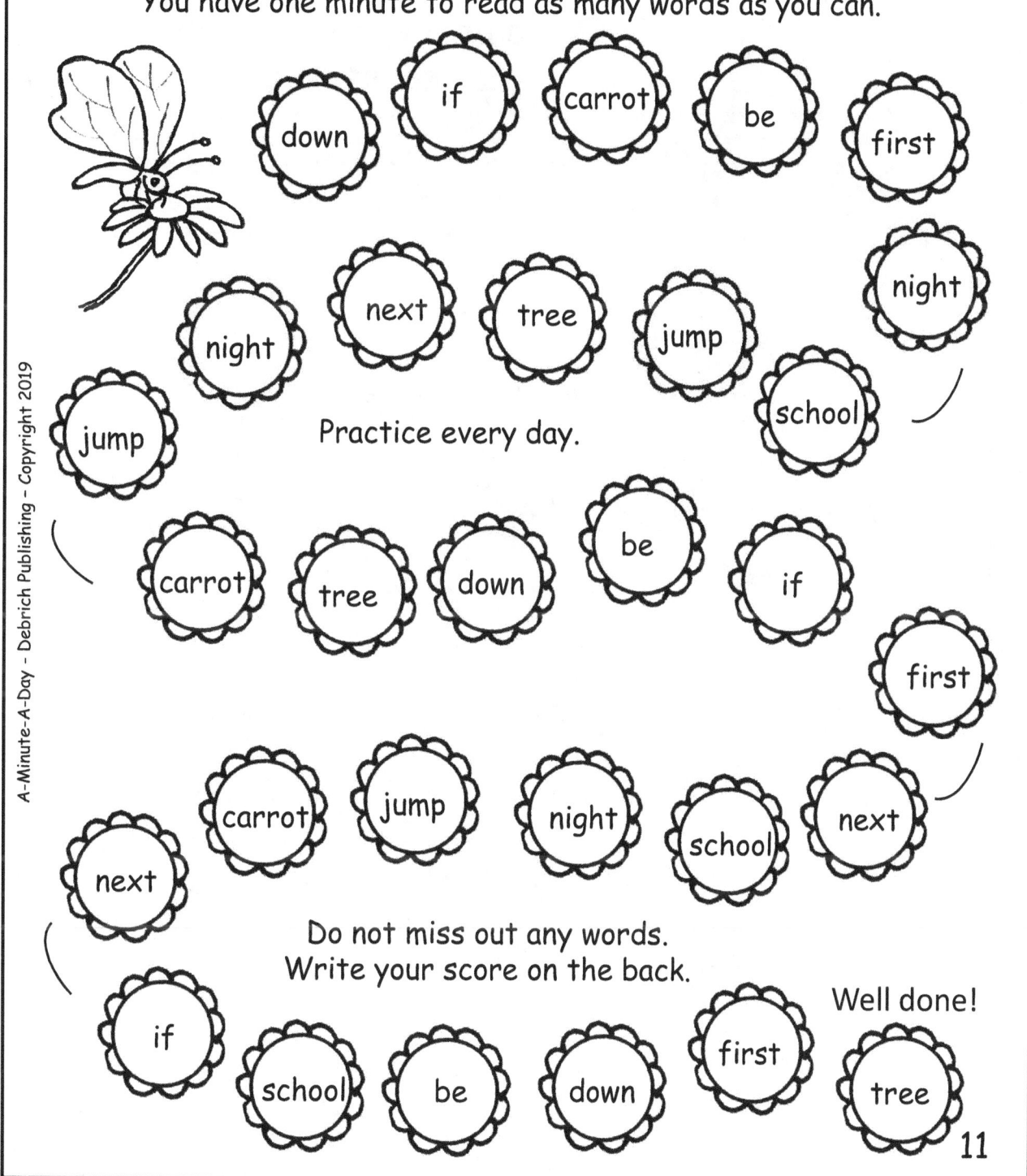

Practice every day.

Do not miss out any words.
Write your score on the back.

Well done!

🎵 Hot Cross Buns 🎵

Hot cross buns!
Hot cross buns!
One a penny, two a penny,
Hot cross buns!

Can you help the baker to sell all his hot X buns?
You may only sell a bun if you can read the word.
You have just one minute to try!

Start seen should because just called

from two lived us not

because seen called not should

from lived us just two

because lived seen should two

just us from not called

All gone!   Practice every day.
Do not miss out any words.
Write your score on the back.

Puddles

Doctor Foster went to Gloucester,
In a shower of rain.
He stepped in a puddle,
Right up to his middle,
And never went there again!

Take care that you don't fall into these puddles!
See how quickly you can read all the words.
You have just 1 minute to read them all!

having good bed last laugh
now say been girl very
good last laugh having bed
very now says girl been
laugh having been last very
good girl bed says now

Practice every day. Do not miss out any words.
Write your score on the back.

Garden Path

Tom's dad has laid a stepping stone path in his garden.
See if you can you read the word on every stone.
You may color a stone when you can read the word.
You have one minute to try!

Start: making → got → boy → little → old → off → so → want → some → water → boy → old → water → off → little → some → making → got → so → want → making → boy → got → little → so → some → want → old → some → so → want → old → water → off → Well done!

Practice every day

Do not miss any words

Write your score on the back.

Party Time

Jan's Mum has made buns for the party.
Can you read the words on every bun,
before they are put into the box.
You have one minute to try!

brother	had	lived	once	way
but	half	love	one	take
live	way	brother	but	had
half	take	love	once	one
once	lived	love	had	way
half	but	one	brother	take

Practice every day.
Do not miss any words.
Write your score on the back.

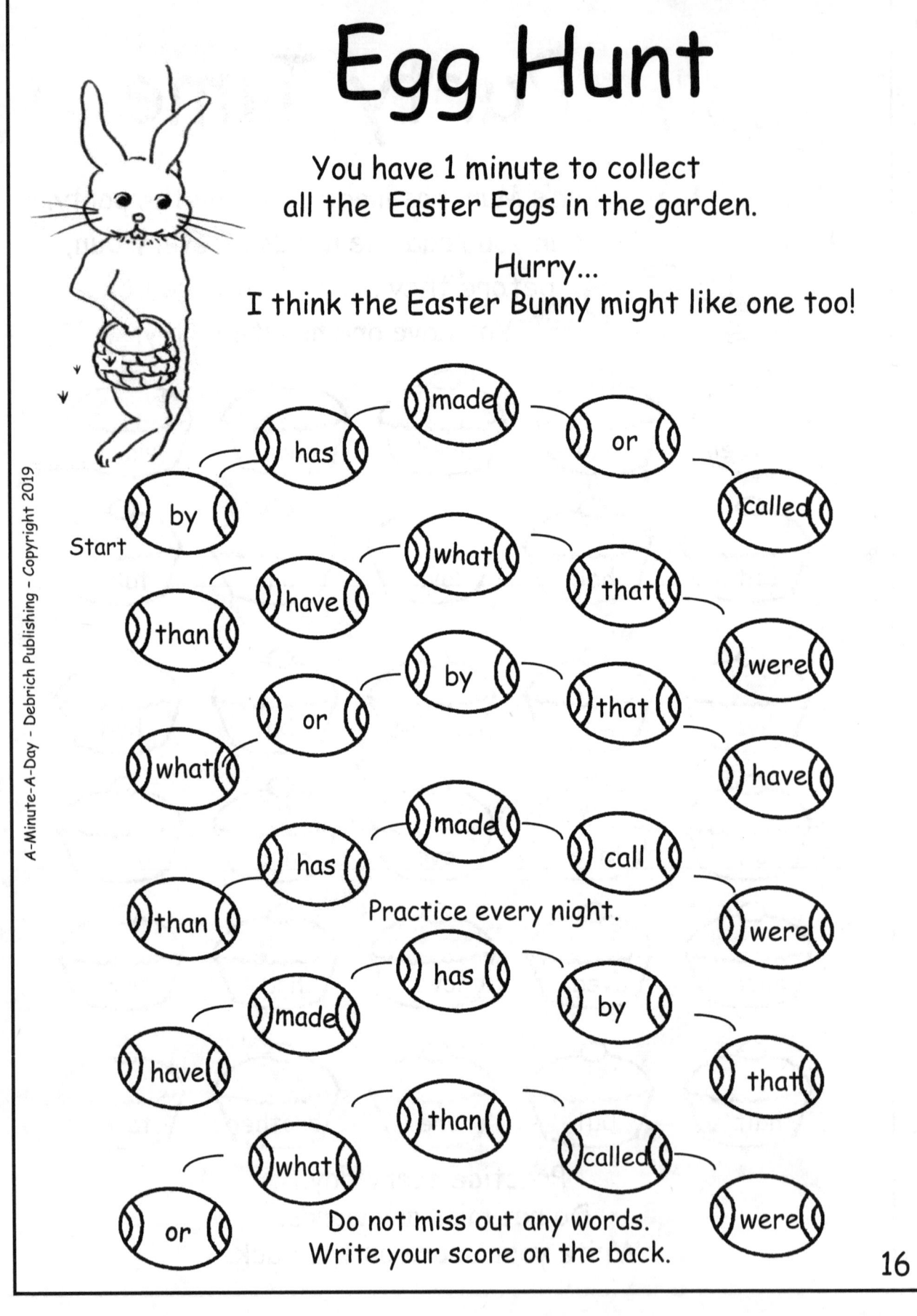

Starlight

Star light, star bright,
The first star I see tonight;
I wish I may, I wish I might,
Have the wish I wish tonight.
How many stars can you read in one minute?

them — our — make — their — when — help

out — came — man — them — make — where

their — when — our — where — help — came

man — out — them — help — make — man

out — where — when — our — came — their

Practice every day.
Do not miss any words.
Write your score on the back.

Snow Storm

It is a windy day.
The snowflakes are falling fast.
Can you read their names
before they are covered by more snow?

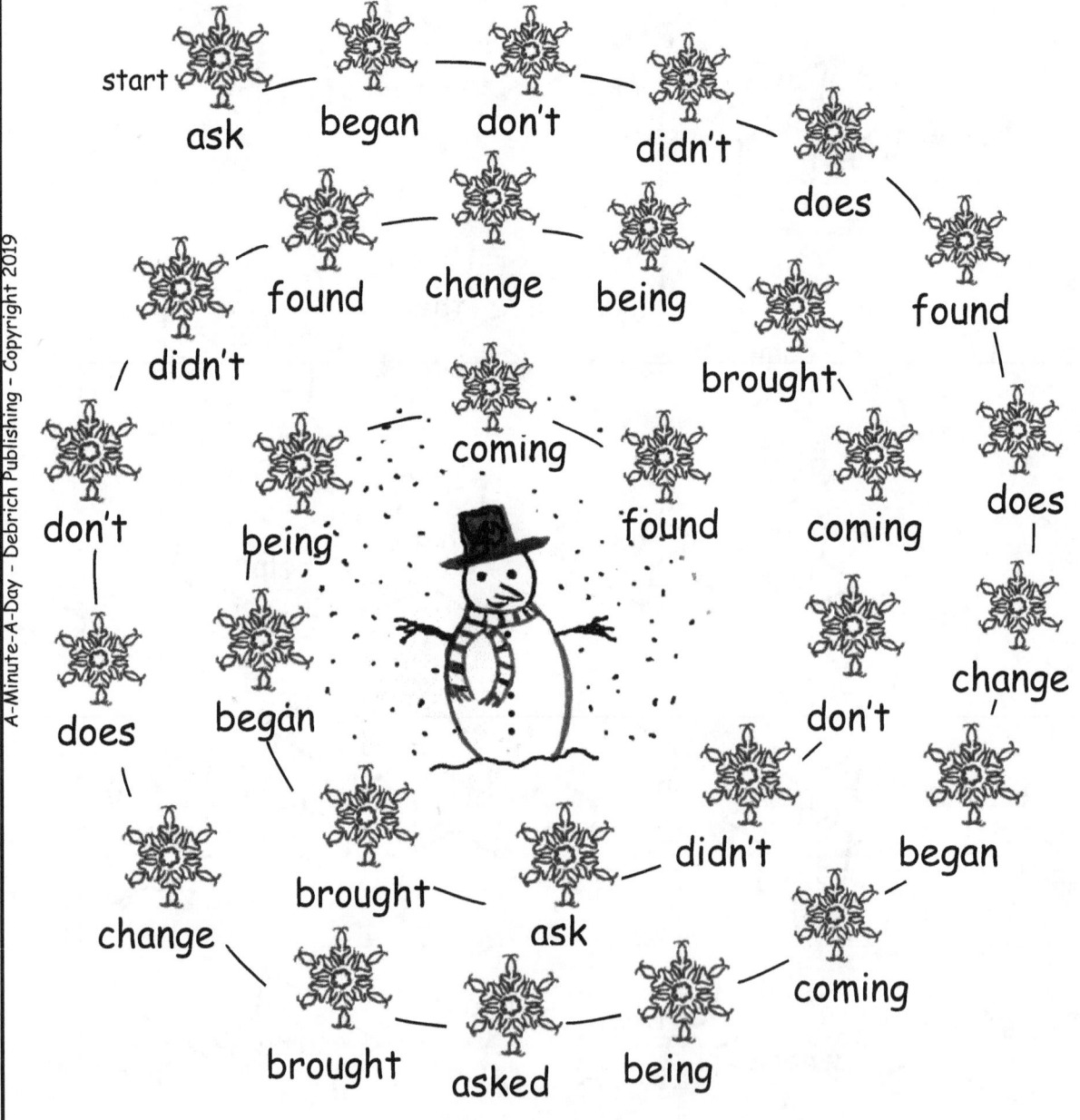

Practice every day.
Do not miss out any words.   Write your score on the back.

Oranges and Lemons

♪♫ Say the bells of St Clement's ♪♫
You owe me five farthings say the bells of St Martin's

Can you read all the words belonging to these oranges and lemons?
You have just one minute to read as many as you can!

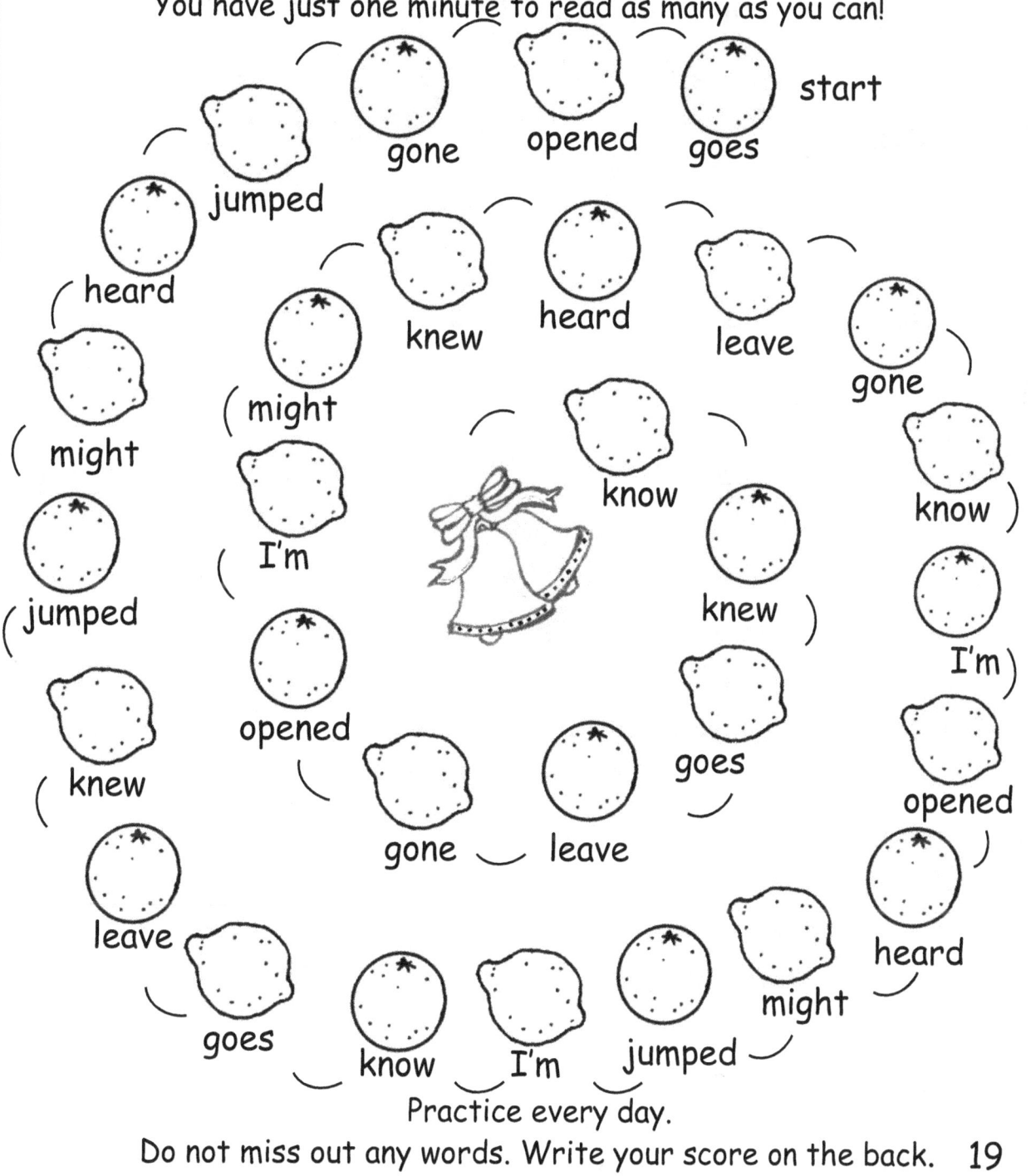

Practice every day.
Do not miss out any words. Write your score on the back.

Build a Wall

Uncle Bill needs lots of bricks to build a wall in his garden. Can you help him to collect the bricks?

You may only pick up a brick if you can read the word on it.

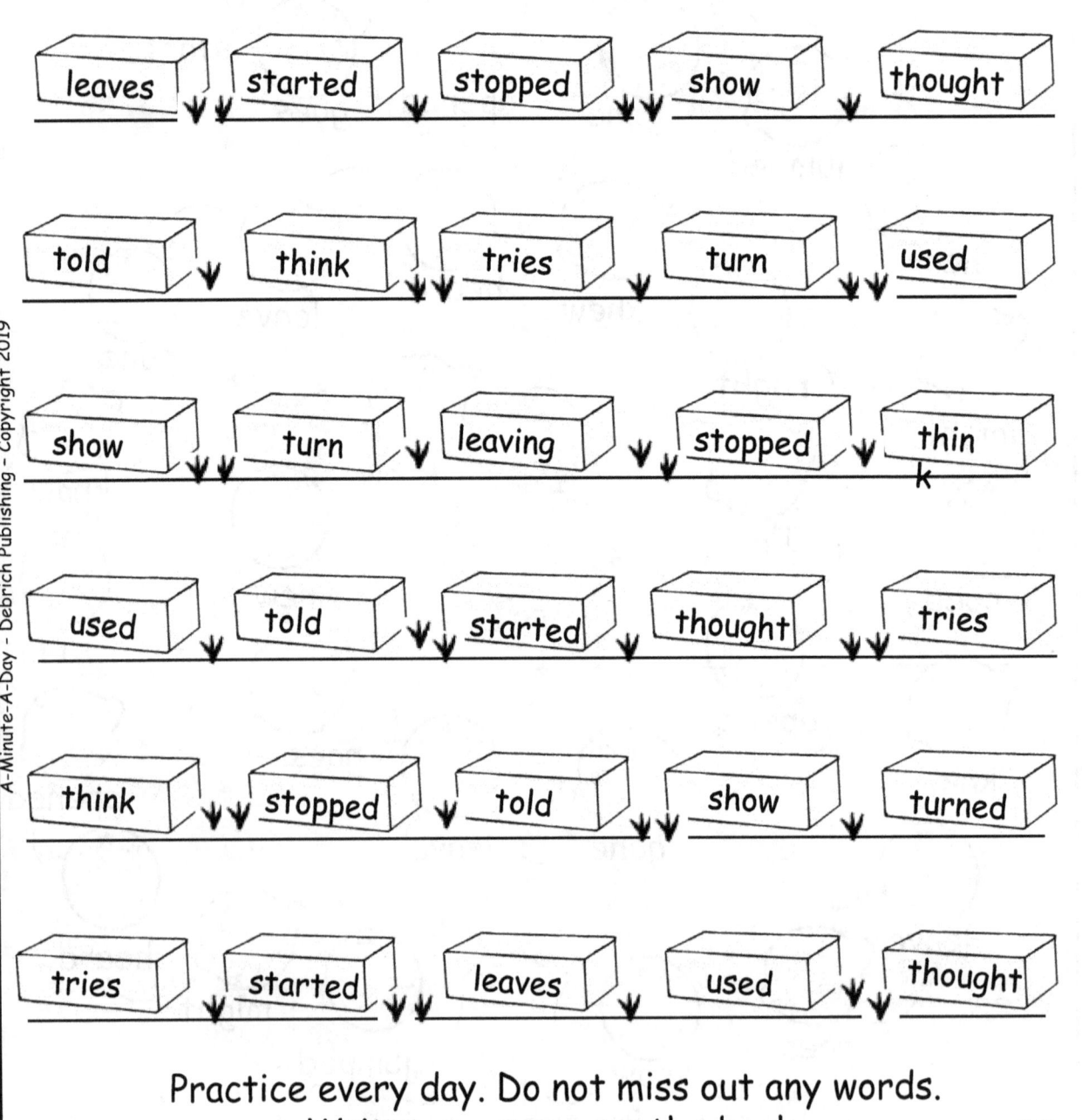

Practice every day. Do not miss out any words.
Write your score on the back.

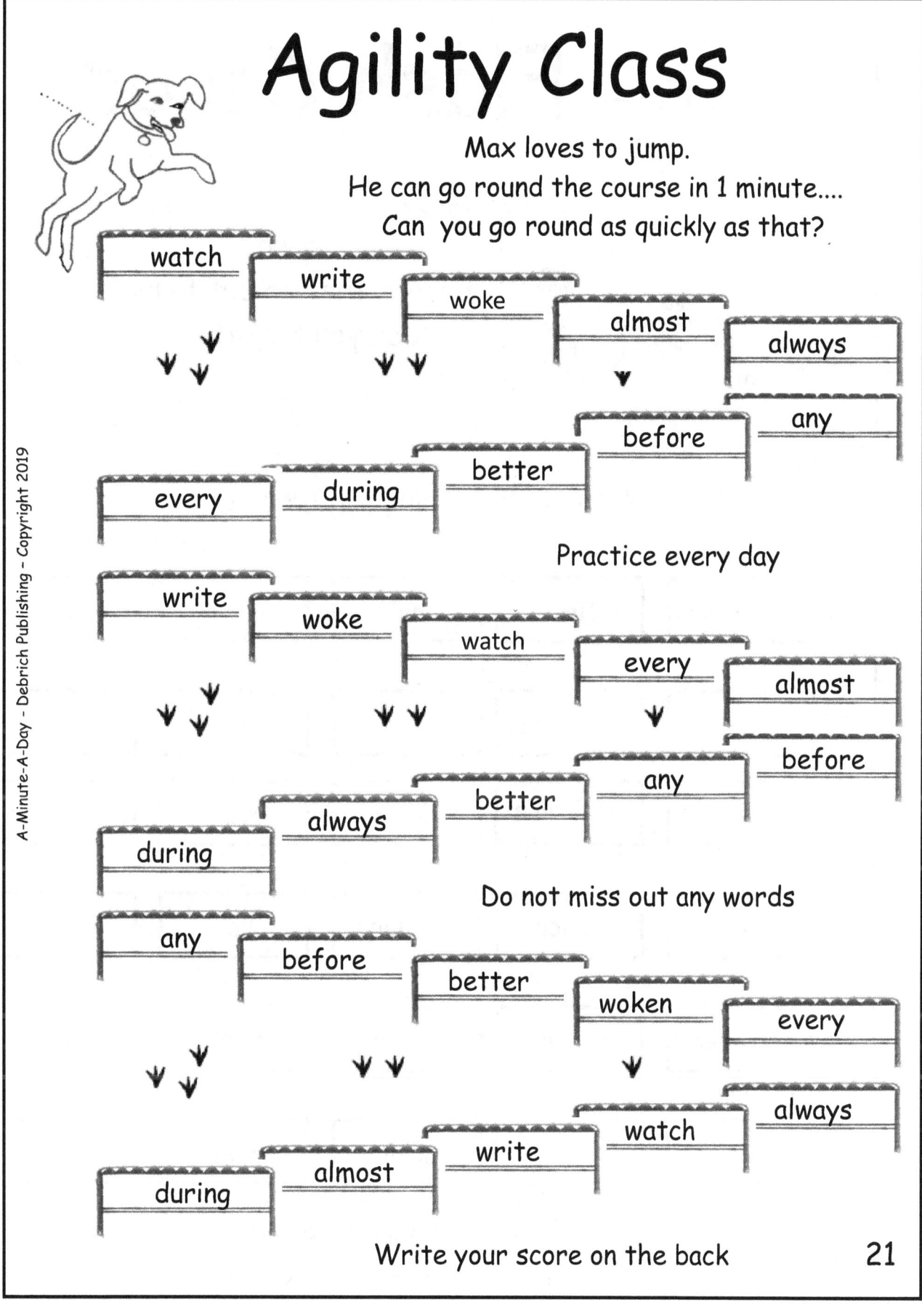

Flash Cards

The children are trying to read all the words
before they go out to play.
Can you help them?

HURRY, the bell will ring in just one minute!

sometimes	first	half	morning	much
never	number	often	only	second
only	sometimes	second	often	number
never	much	morning	half	first
number	never	often	much	only
morning	second	sometimes	half	first

Practice every day. Do not miss out any words
Write your score on the back

Feathers

The robin is collecting feathers
to line her nest.
Can you help her?
You have 1 minute to collect as many as you can.

- still
- suddenly
- today
- until
- upon
- while
- year
- young
- above
- across
- above
- young
- across
- year
- while
- upon
- until
- today
- suddenly
- still
- upon
- while
- until
- today
- year
- young
- suddenly
- above
- still
- across

Practice every day.
Do not miss out any words
Write your score on the back

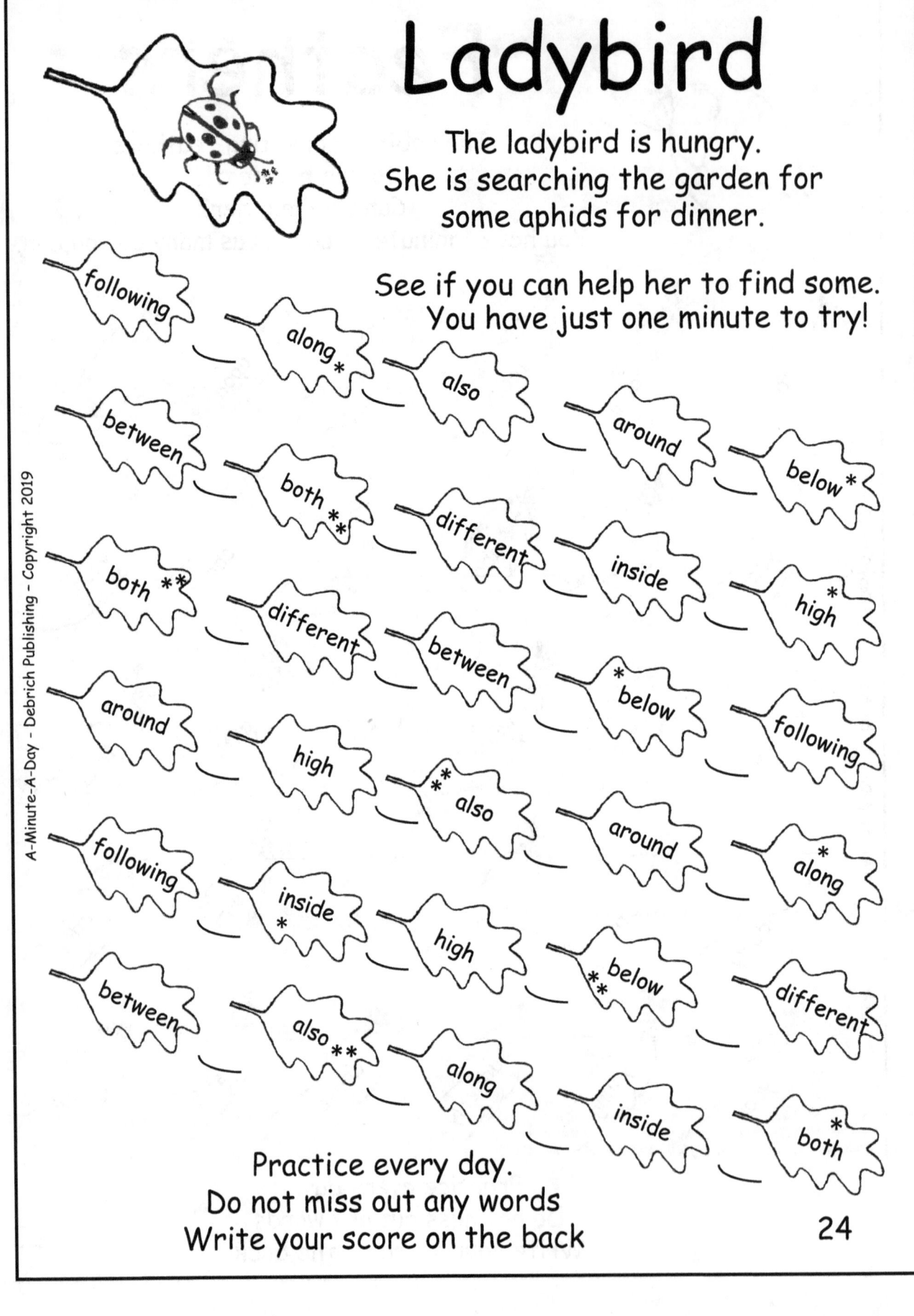

Books

John is searching for a special book.
Can you help him by reading each title?

You have just 1 minute to try.

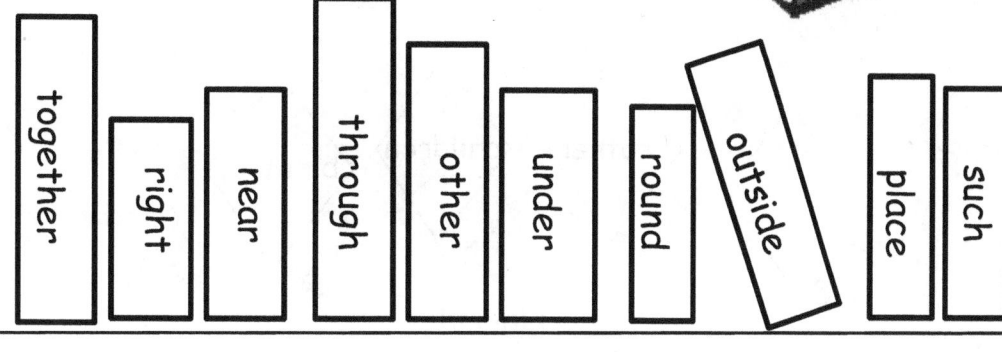

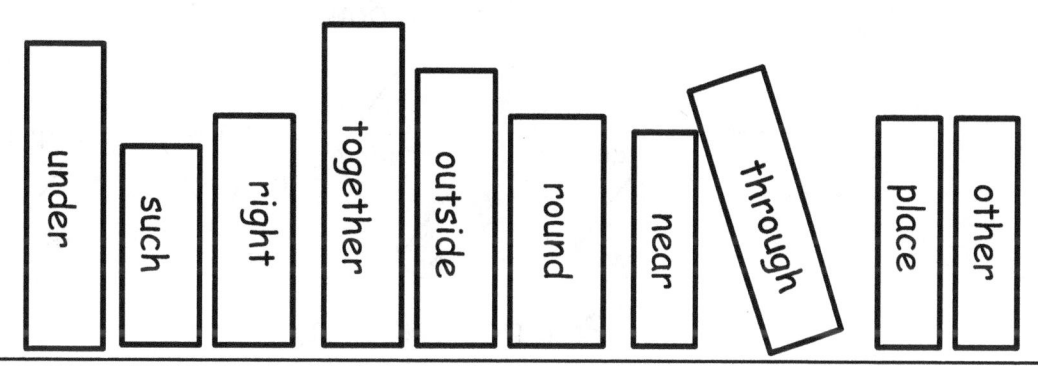

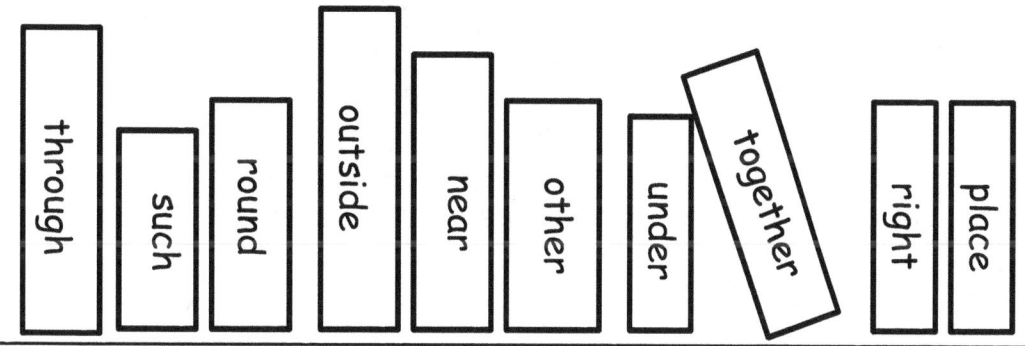

Practice every day.
Do not miss out any words.
Write your score on the back.

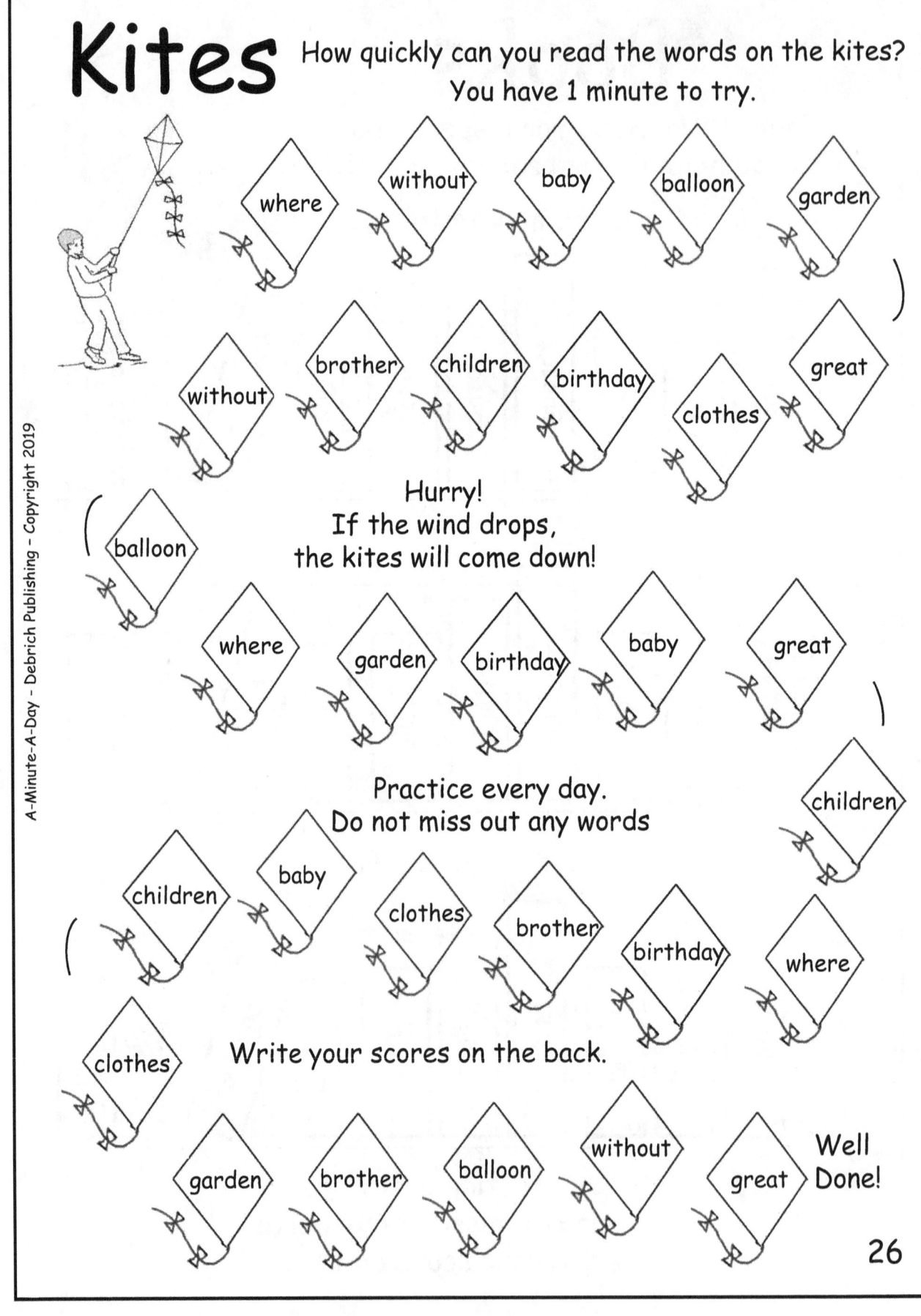

Swallows

The weather is getting cold.
Soon the swallows will fly away to a warm country for the winter.
Can you read the name on each bird before it leaves?

Practice every day. Do not miss out any words
Write your score on the back

Mountain Bike Race

Are you ready?   Draw yourself on the bike ... (Psst don't forget your helmet!)
How many obstacles can you clear in one minute?

earth — light — eyes — money — important — lady — mother — world

friends — money — eyes — father — light — earth — world — friends

important — lady — world — mother — light — eyes — father — money

friends — earth — lady — mother — important — father

1st Champion!

Practice every day. Do not miss out any words.
Write your score on the back.

Scrabble

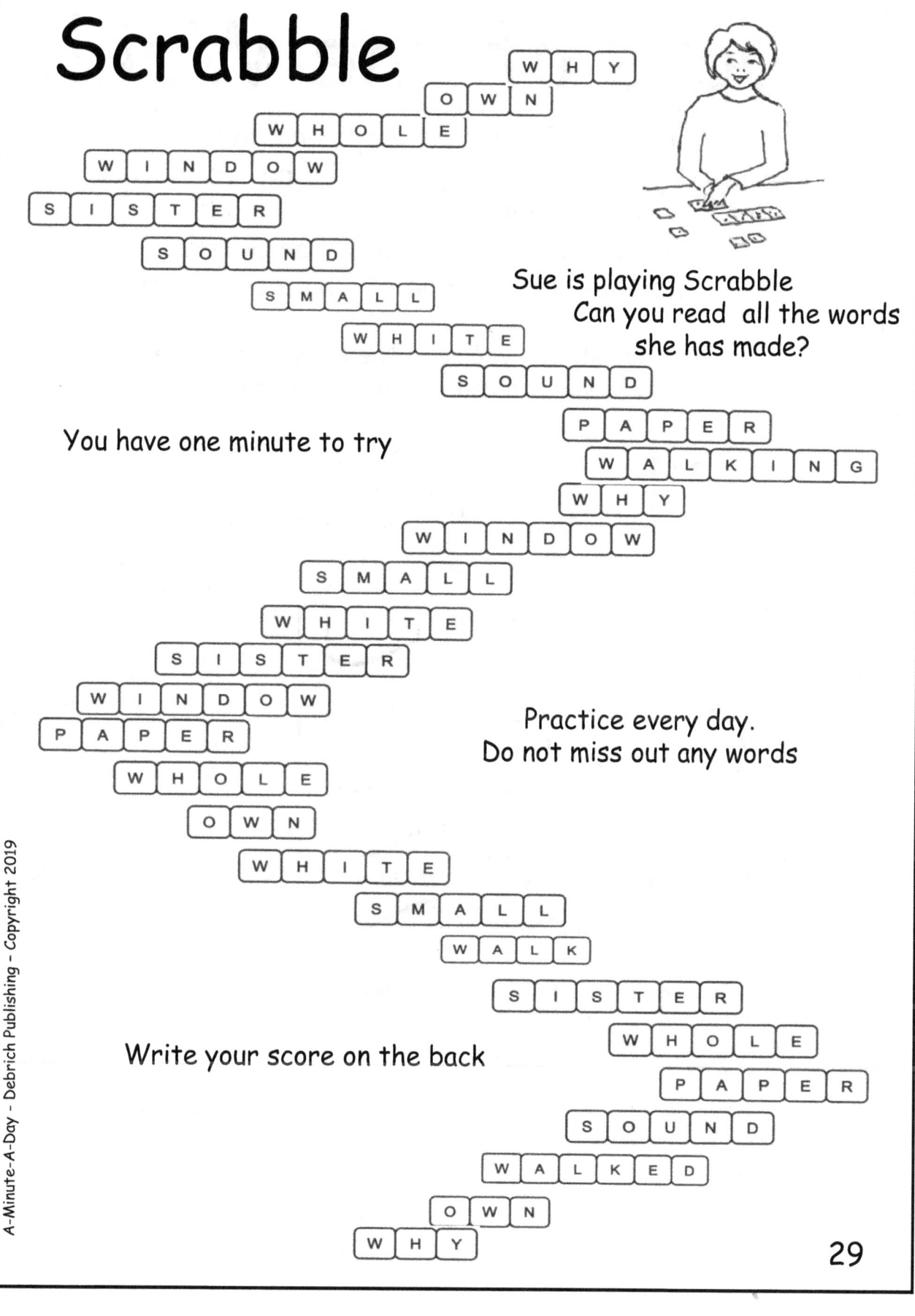

Sue is playing Scrabble
Can you read all the words she has made?

You have one minute to try

Practice every day.
Do not miss out any words

Write your score on the back

29

Days of the Week

Solomon Grundy was born on a Monday,
Christened on Tuesday, married on Wednesday,
Ill on Thursday, worse on Friday,
Died on Saturday, buried on Sunday,
and that was the end of Solomon Grundy!

How quickly can you read the days of the week?
See if you can read them all in one minute.

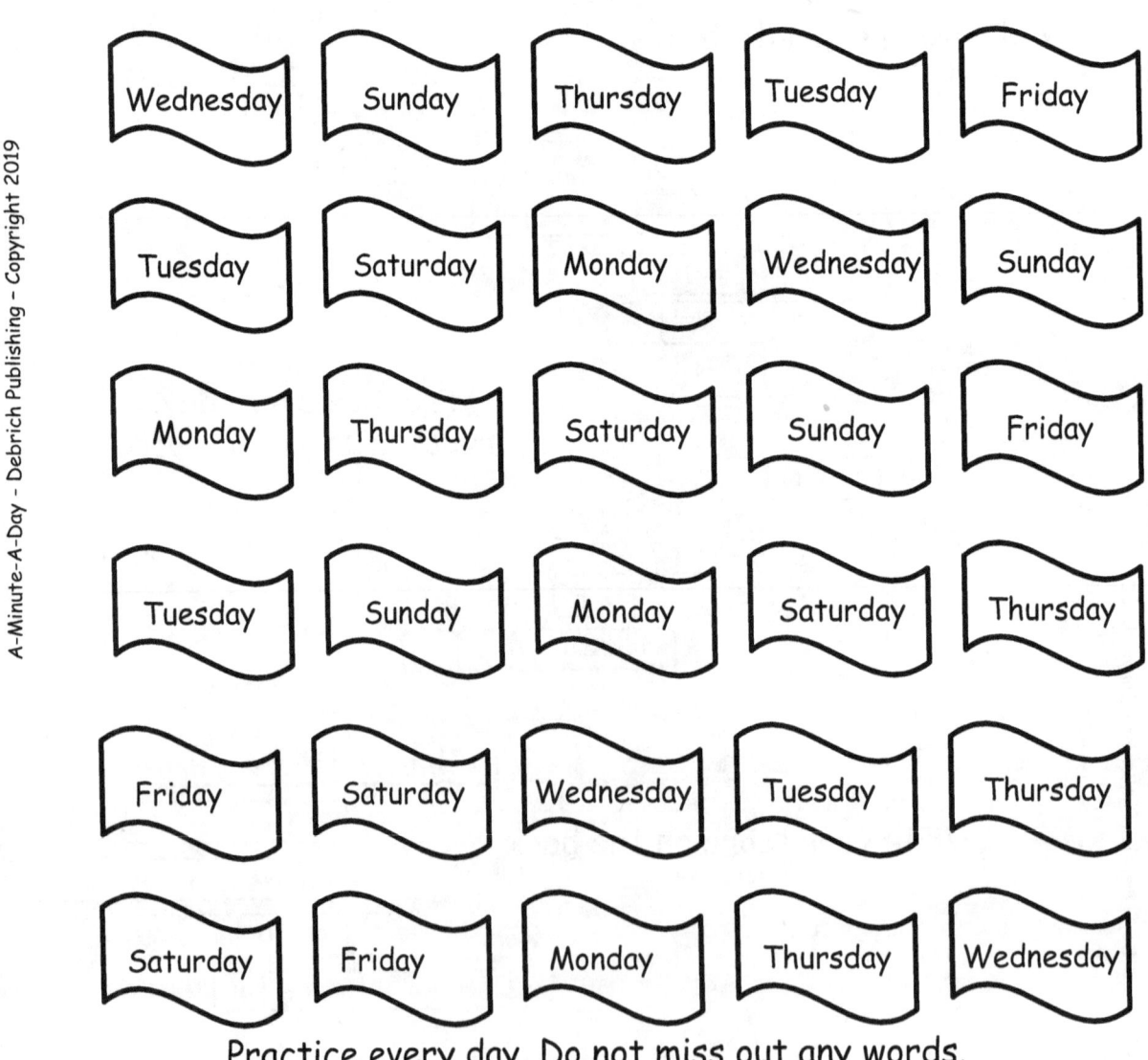

Practice every day. Do not miss out any words.
Write your score on the back.

Months

30 days have September,
April, June and November.
All the rest have 31,
Except for February alone,
which has 28 days clear
and 29 in each leap-year.

Bob has been learning the names of the 12 months of the year.
He can read them all in 1 minute.
Can you beat him?

June	September	August	February	April
October	January	March	November	May
July	December	June	May	February
August	April	September	January	October
May	February	October	April	July
March	December	August	January	November

Practice every day.
Do not miss out any words
Write your score on the back

Numbers 1-10

Do you know this number rhyme?

One, two, three, four, five,
Once I caught a fish alive,
Six, seven, eight, nine, ten,
Then I let it go again

Why did you let it go?
Because it bit my finger so.
Which finger did it bite?
This little finger on the right.

Now see if you can read all these numbers very quickly.
Try to read them all in one minute!

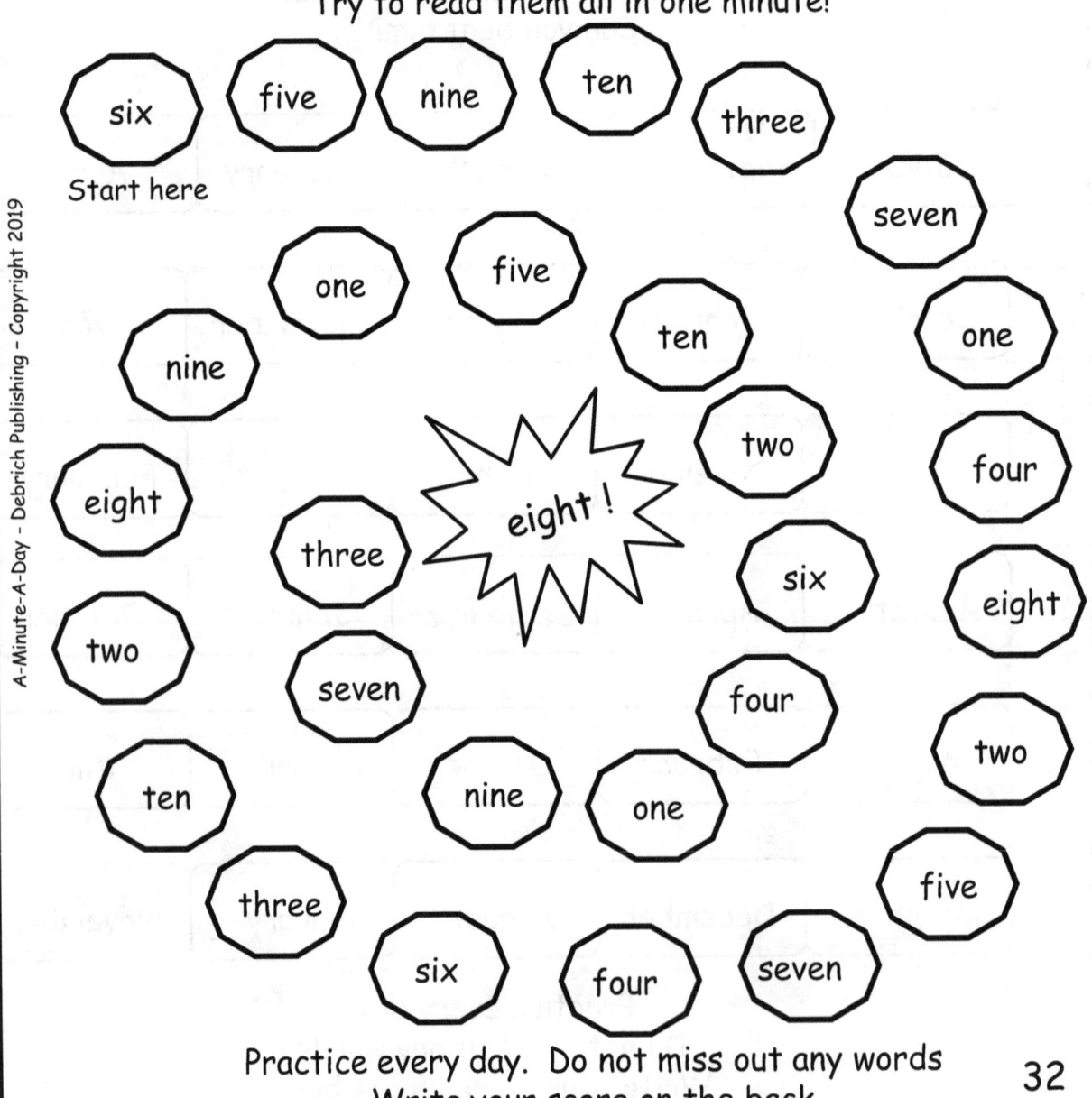

Start here

Practice every day. Do not miss out any words
Write your score on the back

Colors

The children are each allowed to choose a sweet,
if they can read the color on the wrapper.
Can you read the color of every sweet?

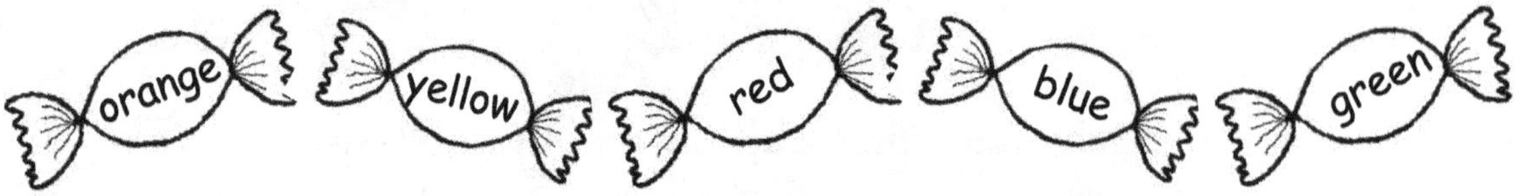

orange yellow red blue green

You have just one minute to try!

purple brown white black pink

yellow purple pink blue brown

Practice every day.

black orange green white red

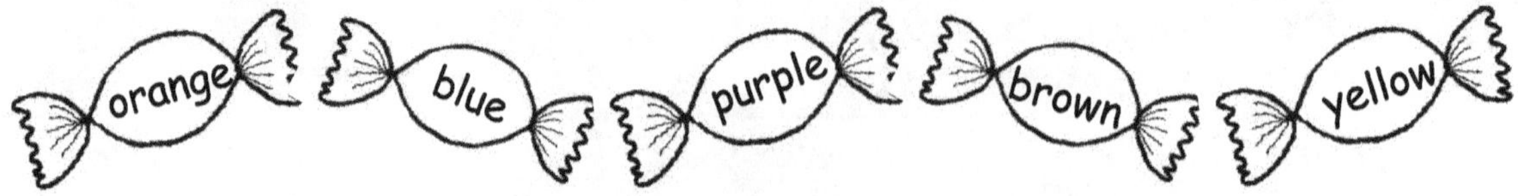

orange blue purple brown yellow

Do not miss out any words

black red pink white green

Write your score on the back

Question Words

The children are visiting the art gallery
They are asking lots of questions.

What is the name of the picture?

Who painted it?

When was it painted?

What kind of paint was used?

How many of these question words can you read?
See if you can read them all in 1 minute.

who?	where?	when?	which?	why?	how?
what?	when?	why?	who?	which?	where?
who?	why?	how?	which?	what?	when?
which?	when?	what?	who?	where?	who?
how?	why?	where?	how?	what?	which?

Practice every day. Write your score on the back

Home Address

This is my address

I am going to practice reading every part of my address. My challenge is to do it all in 1 minute without stopping!

PS Remember to include the zipcode!

Practice every day. Write your score on the back

36

My School Address

All the parts of the address have been jumbled up.
Can you read them all in 1 minute without stopping?

Practice every day.

Do not miss out any words.

Write your score on the back

Hoofprints

The gate is open and the horse has escaped!
Follow the hoofprints to find him.
You may color a hoofprint if you can read the word.
See if you can read them all in one minute.

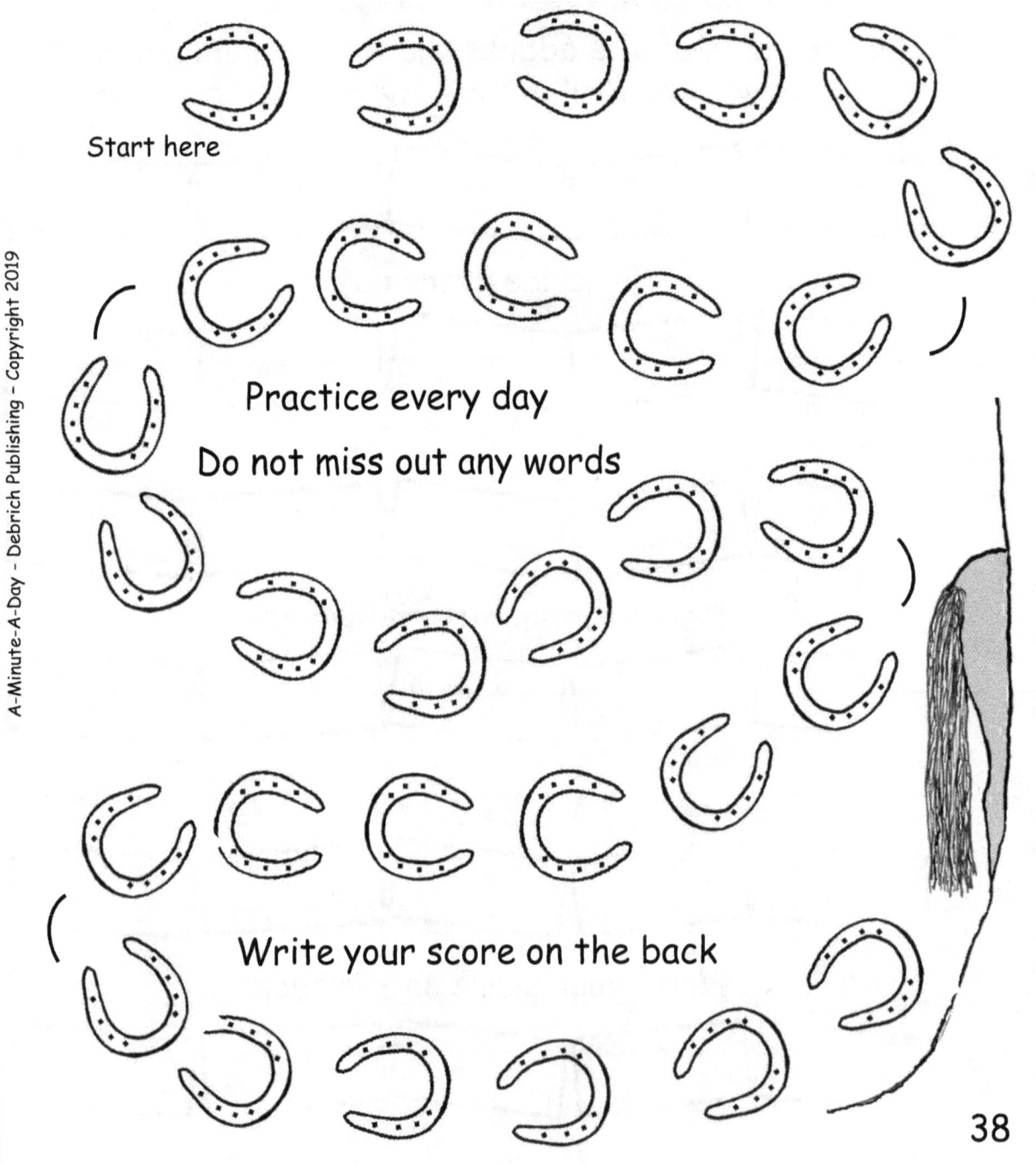

Start here

Practice every day

Do not miss out any words

Write your score on the back

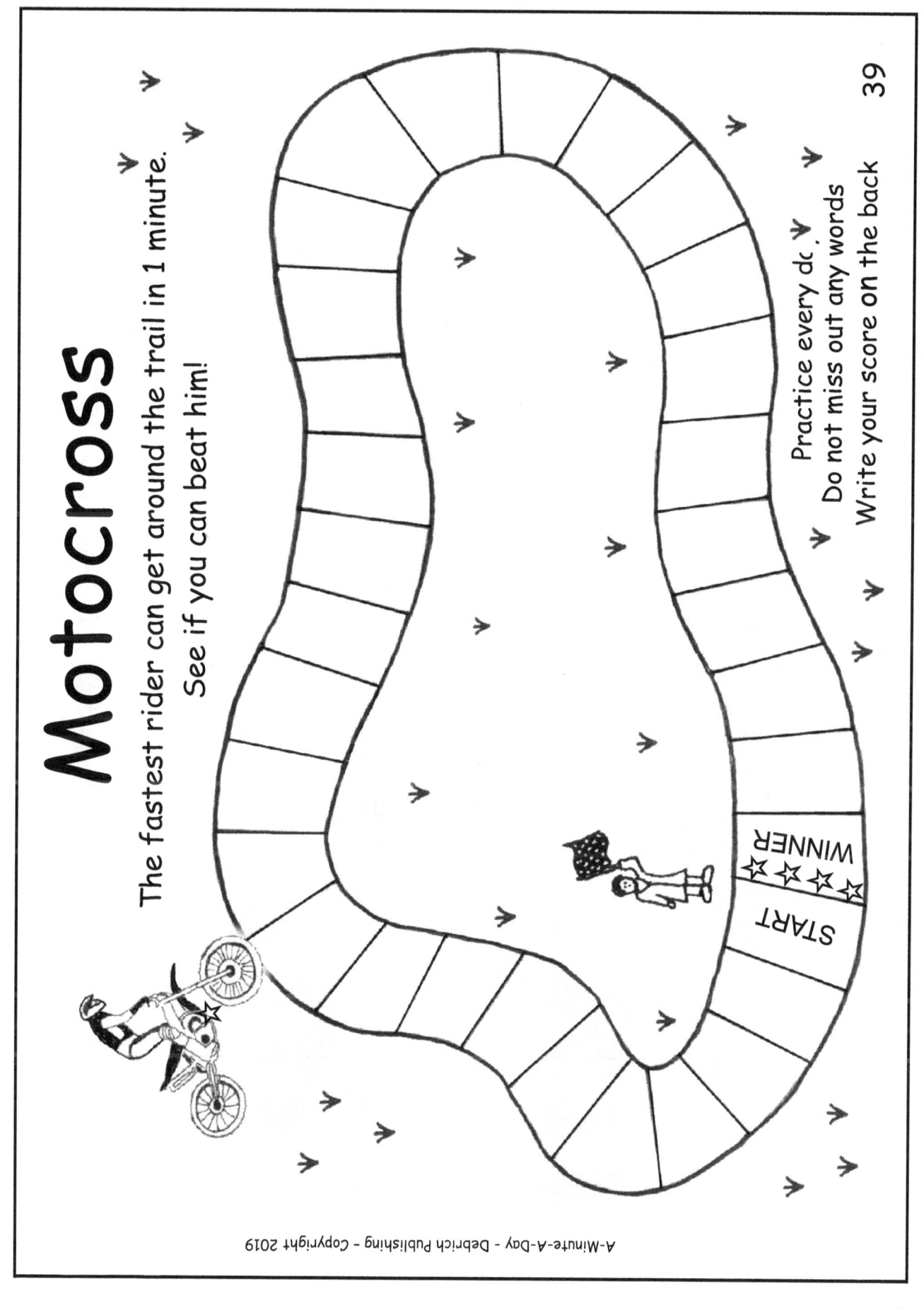

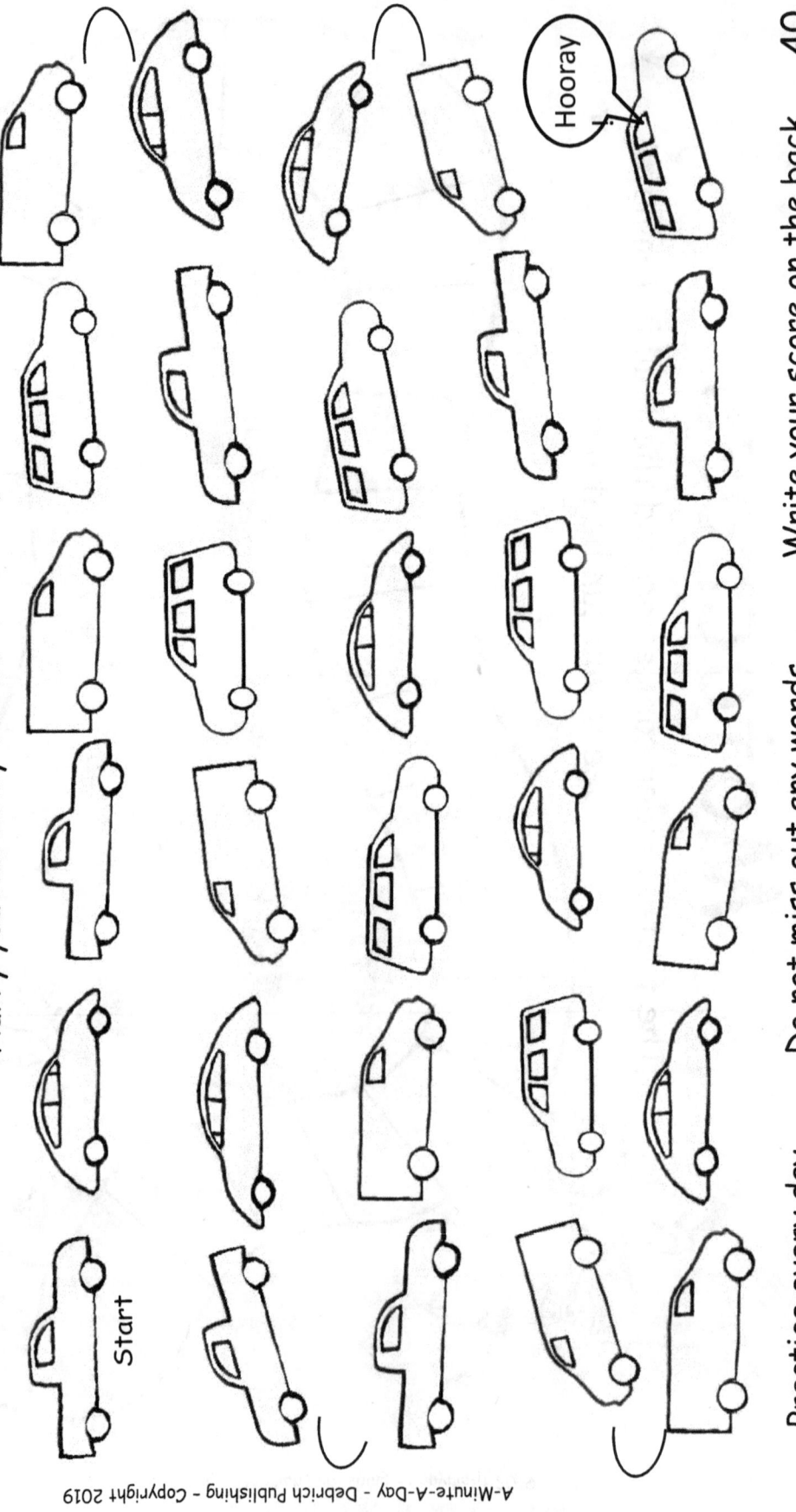

A-MINUTE-A-DAY HIGH FREQUENCY WORDS

Record Sheet (1)

RECEPTION

Start date | Finish date

	Start date	Finish date
1. EGGS I, go, come, went, up, you, day, was, look		
2. BUBBLES are, the, of, we, this, dog, me, like, going		
3. SHELLS big, she, and, they, my, see, on, away, mum		
4. LITTLE DOG it, at, play, no, yes, for, a, dad, can		
5. RAINDROPS he, am, all, is, cat, said, to, in		

YRS 1 - 2

	Start date	Finish date
6. SAVE about, can't, her, many, over, then, who, after, could, here		
7. BALLOON RACE may, people, there, will, again, did, him, more, push, these		
8. DUCK RACE with, an, do, his, much, pull, three, would, another, don't		
9. LUCKY DIP home, must, put, time, your, as, dig, house, name, ran		
10. JAM TARTS too, pocket, back, ball, door, how, new, saw, took, rabbit		
11. BUTTERFLY down, if, next, school, tree, carrot, be, first, jump, night		
12. HOT X BUNS seen, two, lived, because, from, just, not, should, us, called		
13. PUDDLES bed, girl, last, now, say[s], been, very, good, laugh, having		
14. GARDEN PATH making, got, boy, little, old, off, so, want, some, water		
15. PARTY TIME brother, had, live[d], once, way, but, half, love, one, take		

YR 3 and above

	Start date	Finish date
16. EGG HUNT by, has, made, or, that, what, call[ed], have, than, were		
17. STARLIGHT make, our, their, when, came, help, man, out, them, where		
18. SNOW STORM ask[ed], began, being, brought, change, coming, didn't, does, don't, found		
19. ORANGES goes, gone, heard, I'm, jumped, knew, know, leave, might, opened		
20. BUILD A WALL leaves[ing], show, started, stopped, think, thought, told, tries, turn[ed], used		

A-MINUTE-A-DAY HIGH FREQUENCY WORDS

RECORD SHEET (2)

YR 3 and above (continued)

	Start date	Finish date
21. AGILITY CLASS watch, write, woke[n], almost, always, any, before, better, during, every		
22. FLASH CARDS first, half, morning, much, never, number, often, only, second, sometimes		
23. FEATHERS still, suddenly, today, until, upon, while, year, young, above, across		
24. LADYBIRD along, also, around, below, between, both, different, follow[ing], high, inside		
25. BOOKS near, other, outside, place, right, round, such, through, together, under		
26. KITES where, without, baby, balloon, birthday, brother, children, clothes, garden, great		
27. SWALLOWS happy, head, heard, something, sure, swimming, those, word, hear[ing], work [ed] [ing]		
28. BIKE RACE earth, eyes, father, friends, important, lady, light, money, mother, world		
29. SCRABBLE walk [ed] [ing], paper, sister, small, sound, white, whole, why, window, own		
30. DAYS Monday, Tuesday, Wednesday, Thursday, Friday, Saturday, Sunday		
31. MONTHS January, February, March, April, May, June, July, August, September, October, November, December		
32. NOS. 1 -10 one, two, three, four, five, six, seven, eight, nine, ten		
33. NOS. 11 -20 eleven, twelve, thirteen, fourteen, fifteen, sixteen, seventeen, eighteen, nineteen, twenty		
34. COLORS red, blue, yellow, green, purple, orange, brown, black, white, pink		
35. QUESTIONS who, where, when, which, why, how, what		

CONTENT FREE

36. HOME ADDRESS		
37. SCHOOL ADDRESS		
38. HOOFPRINTS		
39. MOTOCROSS		
40. TRAFFIC JAM		

"A-MINUTE-A-DAY" HIGH FREQUENCY WORDS

Dear _____

I am writing to ask for your help with the work _____ is bringing home from school today. *It relates directly to the stage (s)he is focusing upon at school.*

A *maximum* of 15 minutes each day is all that you will need……..about ten minutes to practice and one minute to test, in a room free from distractions such as TV, toys etc.

Do not worry if your child's score is low at the beginning - the emphasis is on *improvement*, i.e. if the score is 6 one night, aim for 8 the next and so on.

Above all……keep the session *brief, light-hearted* and remember to give *lots of praise* for effort.

Would you please write your child's score on the back of the sheet and return it to school every day. Thank you.

Signed ………………………………….

"A-MINUTE-A-DAY" HIGH FREQUENCY WORDS

Dear _____

I am writing to ask for your help with the work _____ is bringing home from school today. *It relates directly to the stage (s)he is focusing upon at school.*

A *maximum* of 15 minutes each day is all that you will need……..about ten minutes to practice and one minute to test, in a room free from distractions such as TV, toys etc.

Do not worry if your child's score is low at the beginning - the emphasis is on *improvement*, i.e. if the score is 6 one night, aim for 8 the next and so on.

Above all……keep the session *brief, light-hearted* and remember to give *lots of praise* for effort.

Would you please write your child's score on the back of the sheet and return it to school every day. Thank you.

Signed ………………………………….

www.ingramcontent.com/pod-product-compliance
Lightning Source LLC
Chambersburg PA
CBHW081502040426
42446CB00016B/3353